Pocket guide to the Scrum Master Certification (PSM 1)

Markus Marfurt

Pocket guide to the Professional Scrum Master Certification (PSM 1)

Markus Marfurt

All information contained in this book has been presented to the best of our knowledge and belief and has been checked several times. Nevertheless, there is always a residual risk that either an error has crept in. Neither the author nor the publisher can be held liable for this.

Impressum

PREFERENTIAL NOTES

Professional Scrum Master ™ (PSM ™) and Professional Scrum Product Owner ™ (PSPO ™) and Professional Scrum Developer ™ (PSD ™) are trademarks of Scrum.org.
This book does not claim any rights to the mentioned trademarks, nor can any guarantees be given for the correctness of the book content. The information provided has been compiled to the best of our knowledge and belief, based on the current state of knowledge. For better readability, the ™ references in the book text have been omitted. However, they are always included.

Bibliografische Information der Deutschen Nationalbibliothek:
Die Deutsche Nationalbibliothek verzeichnet diese Publikation in der Deutschen Nationalbibliografie; detaillierte bibliografische Daten sind im Internet über http://dnb.dnb.de abrufbar.

© 2020 Markus Marfurt

Herstellung und Verlag: BoD – Books on Demand, Norderstedt, Germany

ISBN: 978-3-7519-5751-9

SCRUM AND AGILE 9
AGILE 11
PSM 1 CERTIFICATE AND TESTING 13
Procedure of the test 15
AUDIT STRATEGY 17
Concentrated preparation 17
Focus during the test 18
Preparing documents 18
Read questions completely 19
Schedule two rounds 19
Skip questions - but not completely 20
Keep an eye on the time 20
Use documents that are tailored to Scrum or recommended by Scrum.org 21
Knowledge required to pass the exam 21
Empirism - Empirical basis 23
THE THREE PILLARS OF EMPIRICAL PROCESS CONTROL 25
Transparency 25
Inspection 25
Adaptation 26
THE VALUES OF SCRUM 27

Courage (Courage) 27
Focus 27
Commitment 28
Respect 28
Openness 28
THE SCRUM TEAM 30
The Product Owner 30
The Scrum Master 33
The Development Team 35
SCRUM EVENTS 37
Sprint 37
Sprint Planning 39
   Approach to successful Sprint Planning 40
Daily Scrum 42
Sprint Review 44
Sprint Retrospective 45
SCRUM ARTIFACTS 48
Scrum Artifacts 48
  product backlog 48
  Sprint Backlog 50
  product increase 51
IMPORTANT SCRUM TERMS 53
Product Backlog Refinement 53

Time Box 54
Definition of Done 55
Sprint Goal (optional element) 56
Burn Down Chart 57
TO THE CONCLUSION 58

SCRUM AND AGILE

In most cases, project management is based on the waterfall model (or a comparable approach). This means that before the start of the project or at the beginning of the project, a plan is drawn up for the entire implementation as complete as possible. All conceivable obstacles are taken into account and possible risks are minimized as far as possible. As soon as the project plan is completely prepared, the implementation can begin. In this context, the goal is that the project result predominantly corresponds to what was specified in the underlying planning and the associated requirements documents. The customer (whether internal or external) receives the developed product at the end.

It is an everyday experience that this development approach is associated with considerable risks, especially in the case of projects of longer duration or those with a higher degree of complexity. On the one hand, there is always a certain basic risk as to whether what was originally specified corresponds to what is really needed. Furthermore, there is a risk that the team that has to implement a requirement may understand it in a completely different way than what the client intended. Other challenges include the fact that requirements can change during the course of the project (because the customer needs something else or because certain conditions have changed).

The major weakness of such a development approach is that the customer's involvement during the development period is very low. His knowledge and expertise as a future user are hardly integrated.

Scrum has a completely different approach here. The **framework,** developed by Ken Schwaber and Jeff Sutherland and first presented at the OOPSLA conference in 1995, is based on constant interaction with the customer and his feedback. Since it is based on the exchange and gain of experience through this feedback, it is also called **empirical1**.

The advantages of such an approach are risk and cost reduction.

---

[1] Empirical = based on experience.

AGILE

Agile is based on the Agile Manifesto, which can be found at (www.agilemanifest.org).

Manifesto for Agile Software Development

We are uncovering better ways of developing
software by doing it and helping others do it.
Through this work we have come to value:

Individuals and interactions over processes and tools
Working software over comprehensive documentation
Customer collaboration over contract negotiation
Responding to change over following a plan

That is, while there is value in the items on
the right, we value the items on the left more.

Kent Beck
Mike Beedle

Arie van Bennekum

Alistair Cockburn

Ward Cunningham

Martin Fowler

James Grenning

Jim Highsmith

Andrew Hunt

Ron Jeffries

Jon Kern

Brian Marick

Robert C. Martin

Steve Mellor

Ken Schwaber

Jeff Sutherland

Dave Thomas

The goal was to establish a better way for software development and to define values and principles for it.

The Manifesto, which was published in 2001, was influenced by Scrum among other things, which is also shown by the fact that the two developers of Scrum are also among the first signatories of the Manifesto. Agile is more a philosophy than a method or framework, as is the case with Scrum.

PSM 1 CERTIFICATE AND TESTING

More and more agile development methods and frameworks, also from certificate providers, are coming onto the market and so one might ask why of all things the Scrum certificate should be acquired instead of one of the many others.

The fact that such a large number of people want to acquire the various Scrum certificates - especially the probably best known and most renowned PSM (Professional Scrum Master) certificate - is surely related to the fact that these most likely represent the pure teaching of Scrum and almost all other certificates and approaches can be traced back to it in some way. There are, however, other aspects that make the certificates of scrum.org so highly regarded:

Unlike other certifications, Scrum certificates are not awarded as a bonus for a booked course, but are based solely on an examination conducted by an independent organization (which can also be taken online), in which at least 85% of the questions must be answered correctly. This 85% hurdle represents an additional qualification for certificate holders.

What are the requirements?

- No specific training or course is required to be admitted to the exam.
- If you want to offer courses as an accredited trainer2 , you have to prove many years of Scrum experience as well as pass several exams, which means that corresponding training courses generally have a high level.
- Since the exam is currently only offered in English, a sufficient understanding of the English language is necessary. Especially the technical terms should be present and clear in English.
- The PSM certificate exam only asks for knowledge of the authentic Scrum framework without any other techniques or characteristics.
- The examination fees of currently 150 US$ can be paid online with credit card, Paypal or similar.
- The certification does not expire. A recertification is therefore not necessary.

Procedure of the test

Shortly after the exam is booked online, Scrum.org will send you a receipt as well as the registration confirmation with a password that you have to enter before the exam starts. To be on the safe side, allow for one day. I received the code within a few minutes.

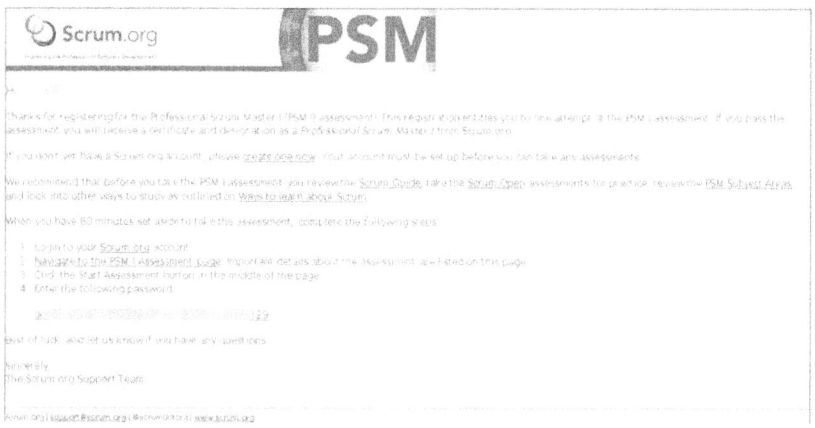

The exam is an "Open Book" exam. It can be taken online on any PC with internet access. Unlike some other exams, video camera surveillance or going to an examination center is not necessary. Currently IE, Chrome and Safari are fully supported as browsers. It is recommended, however, to verify the currently supported browser versions before taking the exam.

15

All questions are checkable. There are questions that have only one answer, questions for which a certain number of correct answers are required, and questions where all correct answers must be ticked. Read the questions very carefully. Among other things, there are also questions for which all "NOT APPLICABLE" answers should be marked.

The test is classified by Scrum.org into an "Intermediate" level. However, this is put into perspective in that with 80 questions within 60 minutes there are only 45 seconds per question available and at least 85% (i.e. 68) questions must be answered correctly in order to receive a certificate.

It is possible to "bookmark" a question and answer or review it at a later time.

If you have a broken connection or other breakdown during the test, please contact (with proof) support@scrum.org.

---

[2] Basically anyone can offer Scrum courses. Please inform yourself about the qualification of the trainer before registration.

AUDIT STRATEGY

In general, proper preparation and strategy contributes a lot to a positive exam result. Below are some of my secrets of success. There is of course the possibility that you are a different type of learner than I am and therefore a different approach might suit you better. Check this out for yourself:

Concentrated preparation

Many people set exams sometime in the future and plan, for example, to take the certification within the next 4 or 8 weeks and prepare themselves accordingly. In the sense of "learning for life", this is in many cases a good strategy because content is repeated over a longer period of time (unless you only start in the last three days before the exam date). If the focus is on certification, I have found that it is easiest for me to schedule the exam at very short notice. If possible, I take a few days before the exam (e.g. on weekends or days off), during which I prepare for the exam from morning to night and then go straight into the exam. This ensures the highest possible level of concentration.

Please make sure, however, that there are no distractions that could prevent you from learning.

Focus during the test

Start the exam when you feel mentally and physically fit. A full stomach that wants to digest is as bad for concentration as a full bladder or thirst. If possible, take the exam at an empty desk with only what you need for the exam (it is an Open Book test, so you can use notes or scripts).

Preparing documents

The fact that 80 questions can be solved in 60 minutes makes it impossible to look up information in a book for long. Accordingly, it is important to prepare documents in a clear and concise manner. Use highlighters and other ways of making texts clearer, or make a note of facts that you absolutely want to keep, but where you see a risk of confusion (for example, the different time boxes for different events, etc.) If you start with documents that you have never read before, you will inevitably be shipwrecked if you want to look up a detail.

Read questions completely

Different questions are often formulated very similarly and there is a risk of overlooking important parts of the question, especially when time is short. Is it possible that somewhere it says "Don't" or "Mark all applicable statements" or is the content of the question negated by a formulation? Only those who read and understand the question completely have a solid basis for a correct answer.

Schedule two rounds

Many people believe that the first solution idea is generally the best and additional errors can occur when looking through answers. However, if you know that your "gut feeling" is generally reliable, then you can take this into account in your considerations during the second run, in case an answer might need to be corrected. During the second round, pay special attention to flagged questions (those where you have set a marker to indicate that you are unsure about the answer) and check again to see if you have really understood the question correctly and if the answer fits the question.

Skip questions - but not completely

The very fact that 85% of the questions have to be answered correctly in order to be certified tempts some people to get stuck on one question and thus spend an enormous amount of time on one point. Be aware that you may answer up to 15% wrong. After all, that's 12 questions. If you haven't found an answer to a question that convinces you after a maximum of two minutes, then mark the most likely answer for you and flag the question. The suggestion to answer the question provisionally is related to the fact that this way you at least have a chance to have answered the question if you do not have enough time at the end. With the flag you can return to "uncertain answers" when all questions have been worked through for the first time and "rack your brains" for the remaining time.

Keep an eye on the time

Especially when you are working concentrated, time can fly by. Take a regular look at the remaining time available and the number of questions left... If you can spare about 40 minutes to answer the first round of questions, that's optimal. You will then have enough time for a second round, in which you can think about questions that are not clear.

Use documents that are tailored to Scrum or recommended by Scrum.org

Many different Agile approaches are very Scrum-like and use both Scrum terms and Scrum-like procedures. Nevertheless, there are usually deviations - even if it is just that the "inventors" want to emphasize an independence. Just because a sprint can take up to 40 or 60 days in any Agile model, this does not necessarily mean that every question in the Scrum exam is judged wrong after the maximum sprint time, which is over 30 days.

Knowledge required to pass the exam

You should be aware that the information in "The Scrum Guide" by Jeff Sutherland and Ken Schwaber is crucial for passing the PSM-1 exam. Any information from authors that deviates from this may mislead you. "The Scrum Guide" can be downloaded in different languages (currently 40) for free at www.scrum.org.

Since many authors who write about Scrum have themselves been working with Scrum for a long time and have adapted the Scrum framework to the needs of their organization, it happens in many works on Scrum that the basics (which are relevant for testing) are mixed with practical experience (which sometimes deviate from the basics). This can lead to confusion and errors during the audit.

The information in this book is strictly based on the content of "The Scrum Guide" and the author assumes that you have already read the guide. In practice it is often the case that the Guide contains all the necessary information, but many readers find it difficult to draw conclusions about the exam questions from the statements contained in the Guide. This is exactly where this book comes in.

On the Internet there are various providers of test tests, which are sometimes offered for horrendous money. Basically it can be said that such tests do not correspond to reality in many cases and in some cases even give wrong answers. On the website of Scrum.org there is an Open Assessment where a free test exam with 30 real test questions can be taken. The questions are randomly arranged and selected from a part of the real exam questions. For all other test exams you should always ask yourself where they come from and how trustworthy and competent the respective provider is.

With regard to the Open Assessment, it should be noted that it only contains basic questions that appear on the exam, but that the exam itself is more difficult. It is recommended that you only take the real exam if you have taken the Open Assessment exams several times in a row in less than 10 minutes and have answered 100% of the questions correctly.

In the following chapters I will try to present the content of the Scrum Guide in a way that ensures optimal exam preparation. Since the exam is held in English, the basic terms are in English and for example "Development Team" (role in Scrum) and not "Developer Group" is used.

Empirism - Empirical basis

Traditional development approaches are usually based on the idea that all requirements are recorded in detail in the form of specifications, requirement and functional specifications before the project begins and that the developers should then implement the described functions at a certain point in time. This also works best if the requirements are actually met by the customer (internal or external), if the developers understand them as they were meant by the writers of the specifications, and if the customer's requirements do not change during the development process. However, reality shows that this cannot be assumed in every case. This is one of the reasons why a large number of development projects are either never completed or have to be reworked with (sometimes considerable) additional effort.

Scrum is based on a different approach. This is called empirical because it is based on experience and continuously adapts the development process to facts, experiences and feedback from the practice.

THE THREE PILLARS OF EMPIRICAL PROCESS CONTROL

The further development of a system or product based on experience is only possible if some basic principles are in place. These include basic rules (also called "Three Pillars of Empiricism" or "Key Factors of Scrum Theory") as well as a basic set of values.

Transparency

Experience-based development requires an open corporate culture. Where employees or superiors hide mistakes and pursue hidden goals that compete with the project goal, experience-based development is not possible. Transparency requires a basic mutual trust, which allows to stand by mistakes and to make the lessons learned available to other team members. Transparency is only possible if it is lived company-wide.

Inspection

Inspection in the Scrum context does not mean monitoring or testing by external inspectors or auditors. Rather, the inspection takes place as part of the Scrum process, both within the team and in contact with the client. The results of each sprint (increment) are shown to the customer and are reviewed and checked together with him. Even if a customer wishes changes in one of these reviews compared to previously expressed ideas, a Scrum team sees this as an opportunity to achieve even greater benefits for the customer.

Adaptation

Adaptation is to be seen as part of the continuous improvement process. On the one hand, this means the adaptation of product improvements based on the results of the "inspection". Adaptation, however, is undoubtedly also to be seen in the context of the Sprint retrospective. The knowledge gained in this process also leads to an adaptation of the procedures within the development team, but possibly also in the entire Scrum Team.

THE VALUES OF SCRUM

A new approach to collaboration, as Scrum was at least at the time of its development, but for some companies that are new to Scrum, is still today, is always based on certain values. In the case of Scrum the 5 values are called "Courage", "Focus", "Commitment", "Respect", "Openness".

Courage (Courage)

The members of the Scrum team need the courage to work on the right things. They show courage for transparency and are willing to take risks. They accept challenges and show the courage to always look for even better solutions and ways of resolution in order to deliver even better results. You stand by mistakes and are committed to continuous improvement.

Focus

The members of the Scrum team are focused on achieving the agreed goals. The work in time boxes focuses on producing executable software that meets the needs of the customers, so that one does not get lost in unimportant details.

Commitment

The members of the Scrum team are characterized by a strong commitment to the jointly agreed goals. They uphold the principles outlined in the Agile Manifesto. The team is committed to developing executable software of the agreed quality, to collaboration, transparency, personal and team development, self-organization and working within the Scrum framework.

Respect

The members of the Scrum team respect each other as capable and independent people. They show respect for people and respect their differences. They respect roles, rules and principles of Scrum. They show respect for their customers by perceiving their needs as the goal of their software development and by bringing their product closer to the customers' needs with every sprint.

Openness

Scrum Team and the involved stakeholders are committed to open communication within the team, but also with all other involved parties. Openness and transparency is understood as a basic requirement for the optimal achievement of the set goals.

THE SCRUM TEAM

The Scrum team consists exclusively of the following three roles:

- Product Owner
- Scrum Master
- Development Team (mit 3-9 Developern)

Other roles may exist in a company, but they are not part of the Scrum team.

The task of management in the Scrum context is to provide the Product Owner with the necessary information that enables him to perform his tasks optimally and to support and strengthen him in his role and task. In particular, management must not try to circumvent the Product Owner in any way and, for example, position requirements directly with the development team.

The Product Owner

- The Product Owner is responsible for the Product Backlog. He arranges the tasks in it in such a way that the development team can start with those that bring the most

benefit. Criteria can include their benefits, commercial impact, dependencies, importance to the customer, impact on costs.
- The Product Owner ensures that all requirements implemented by the development team come from a single product backlog.
- The Product Owner keeps the vision of the end result high and thus offers the development team a clear orientation. He is also responsible for understanding and internalizing the customer's needs.
- Its task is to maximize the value of the resulting product. To do this, he informs himself about all aspects of the product and its future benefits, about its costs, its amortization, etc.
- The product owner ensures that increments are released regularly in order to be able to test customer benefits in practice.
- The Product Owner is always an individual. However, he can work with a committee that supports and advises him.
- The product owner has the competence to decide on his own. Only in this way can delays be avoided. He decides independently on the inclusion of elements in the product backlog and their arrangement.
- To do so, it must be accepted by the Scrum team, but also within the organization and by customers. No attempts may

be made to override it. But it can certainly support the dialog (e.g. to clarify issues) between the development team and the customer.
- Even if several development teams work on a product, there is only one product backlog and one product owner. For such projects Scrum.org has defined its own approach with the Nexus framework. The certification "Scaled Professional Scrum" is available for this.
- The product owner works out the acceptance criteria together with the development team.
- The Product Owner ensures that the Development Team has all the information they need to successfully implement the PBI (tasks). To this end, he coordinates with all relevant sources.
- Since the development team can also take on tasks that are already listed in the product backlog but have not yet been finally specified, questions are clarified further during the sprint.
- The Product Owner is responsible for the costs. This refers to both development costs and future maintenance costs and costs arising from the use.
- The Product Owner is the only role that has the right to stop a sprint if its content has become obsolete. Functions that have already been fully implemented are usually transferred

to the solution. Tasks that have not yet been fully completed are returned to the product backlog, where they are re-evaluated and reassessed if necessary.
- If the development team discovers that it has taken on too many tasks for a sprint, it will decide together with the product owner how to proceed.
- The existence of a Product Owner is a prerequisite to work according to Scrum.
- The Product Owner must make a 100% commitment to the Scrum Team. Depending on the constellation, the Product Owner can also be a member of the Development Team as long as his tasks as Product Owner are not affected.

The Scrum Master

- The central task of the Scrum Master is to build and develop a successful Scrum Team (or merere).
- He is a coach, teacher and mentor. His task is to remove obstacles and simplify the tasks for the team. He is at the same time leader and servant of the team and does his job without fuss.

- His task is to eliminate incidents that prevent the Scrum team from functioning optimally. For this purpose he coaches and trains the Scrum Team so that they can remove obstacles themselves. Where it cannot do this, the Scrum Master takes over the corresponding task.
- The Scrum master is responsible for ensuring that Scrum is understood and used. To do so, he informs both the Scrum team and the organization and builds on the Scrum topic wherever it makes sense.
- The Scrum Master supports the development team and the product owner in case of communication difficulties.
- The Scrum Master ensures that a Daily Scrum takes place every day. He does not have to participate himself.
- The presence of a Scrum Master is a prerequisite to work according to Scrum.
- The Scrum Master must be available for the Scrum Team (100% commitment), but can work in several Scrum Teams or as a member of the Development Team, as long as this does not limit his tasks as Scrum Master and his availability when needed.

The Development Team

- The Development Team organizes and manages itself.
- There are no specific roles within the team (e.g. tester). All team members have the same responsibilities and status as "Developer".
- The development team ideally consists of 3-9 members. With a larger or smaller number, productivity can suffer.
- The development team selects the number of tasks (PBI - Product Backlog Items) that the Product Owner considers feasible, based on the Product Owner's instructions. There must be no external influence or even assignment to implement certain tasks.
- The development team takes responsibility for the selected tasks during the sprint as a team.
- It is responsible for creating a potentially releasable program version (releasable increment) at the end of the sprint. Only what meets the acceptance criteria 100% will be included in this program version. Everything else flows back into the product backlog.
- The Development Team is responsible for the quality of the increase as a whole. The task solutions delivered in an

Increment must all comply with the D.O.D. (Definition of Done = acceptance criteria).

- The Development Team creates and is responsible for the acceptance criteria itself (if necessary, supported by the Product Owner during creation).
- The development team must have all the skills needed to independently solve the tasks arising in the sprint.
- The development team decides for itself how the work in the team is organized during the sprint.
- It resolves internal conflicts itself (if necessary with the help of the Scrum Master).
- The development team estimates the effort required for the various PBI.
- In case of direct orders or inquiries to the development team, the team refers to the product owner.
- Members of the development team can be replaced at any time if necessary. It should be noted that this may result in a short-term reduction in performance. Ideally (but not necessarily) a change should take place at the end of a sprint.
- If several Scrum teams - and thus several development teams - work on the same product backlog, the productivity of the individual teams is reduced through additional coordination and integration efforts.

SCRUM EVENTS

Scrum knows five formal events, where the sprint contains the other events. All events are time-boxed (they have a fixed duration). Each event is a formal opportunity for inspection and improvement. It enables transparency and continuous improvement. If the events are not executed properly, transparency is reduced and it is a missed opportunity for improvement.

Sprint

- A sprint is a time-boxed event in Scrum. The maximum duration is 1 month.
- Relevant for the duration of the sprints is the frequency of new requirements, the degree of risk and how often interaction and verification of the results by the client is necessary for the team.
- Its goal is to produce a usable and potentially releasable product that meets the "Definition of Done".
- As soon as one sprint is finished, the next one starts (there is a pause between them).

- A sprint can be started even if the tasks to be processed have not yet been finally defined. In this case, the tasks are defined in cooperation with the product owner during the sprint to the extent required by the development team.
- A single sprint can also be seen as a separate project with a fixed duration of 1 month.
- If the sprint target becomes obsolete, the product owner can cancel a sprint early. Functions that have already been implemented at the time of abort are taken over into the increment, all others fall back into the product backlog.
- The time-boxed should be constant over a project. This is the only way the development team can select the optimal number of tasks for each sprint based on their experience.
- The fixed duration of a sprint must never be exceeded (not even to complete any other tasks).
- If sprints of more than one month were chosen, the complexity and risk would increase and the focus on the implementation of the requirements defined in DoD would suffer.

Sprint Planning

- Sprint Planning is the first of the events included in the Sprint.
- In it, the whole Scrum team decides together which tasks from the Product Backlog are selected for the sprint for implementation.
- The meeting is time-boxed with a maximum of 8 hours for a monthly sprint. For shorter sprints the meeting is shortened accordingly.
- Results of the Sprint Planning Meeting are the answers to two questions:
    - Which tasks (Product Backlog Items) are implemented in the Sprint? These are transferred to the Sprint Backlog.
    - How is this goal to be achieved? The tasks included in the Sprint Backlog are based on an effort estimate for each task. The elements contained in the Sprint Backlog should be implemented in the Sprint and, if the criteria in the D.o.D. are met, they should be included in the next increment.

The roles and tasks in the Sprint Planning Meeting

- The Sprint Planning Meeting should be attended by the entire Scrum team.
- If necessary, the Scrum team can call in external experts to provide information (whether technical or professional) needed for the work.
- The Scrum Master supports (facilitate) the meeting. But also other Scrum Team members can make their contribution.
- The product owner represents the business focus. He answers questions about the PBI (Product Backlog Items). The development team discusses deviations in the implementation sequence with him if a task is skipped that, according to its arrangement in the product backlog, is no longer available for any reason (dependencies, effort no longer fits into the sprint...).

Approach to successful Sprint Planning

Basically, there are different approaches, which all correspond to the Scrum Framework. One approach in three steps has proven to be particularly effective:

Advance planning

The Scrum team ensures that all potentially relevant PBIs are already defined and ready before the Sprint Planning Meeting. This includes:

- that they are arranged in the product backlog in the order of their importance and value
- that the acceptance criteria are clearly formulated (Acceptance Criteria)
- that a rough estimate of the effort required for the individual tasks is available.

This can be achieved by holding Refinement Meetings during the previous Sprint Product Backlogs, in which the points mentioned above were worked out.

Task per task

The development team analyzes one product backlog item after another and divides them into individual tasks, which are also estimated individually. Based on the capacity of the Development Team, Product Backlog Items are transferred to the Sprint Backlog using these estimates.

Implementation

During the implementation process, additional questions arise and it is possible that the resulting answers may also result in significant deviations from the effort estimates. As a result, it may be necessary not to implement certain PBIs or to include additional PBIs in the Sprint. Both are done in consultation with the product owner. In principle, it is sufficient to have sufficient information for the first few days to start the work of a sprint. If necessary, all further information can be worked out and clarified during the sprint.

Daily Scrum

Daily Scrum is a daily recurring event in Scrum. It always takes place at the same time and place to reduce additional complexity and coordination efforts. Participants are the development team, other people can participate as observers (transparency), but do not have an active role. The goal of the Daily Scrum is to coordinate the work for the next 24 hours. The Scrum Team is time-boxed 15 minutes (independent of the length of the sprint).

In the Daily Scrum each member of the development team answers the following three questions:

1. What have I completed since the last meeting?
2. What will I finish by the next meeting?

3. What obstacles / challenges do I see on the way there?

All further discussions, such as approaches to solutions, but also further exchange of ideas will take place after the Daily Scrum. The team members' answers to the three questions allow the progress of the implementation to be measured and presented. A burndown chart is usually used for this purpose.

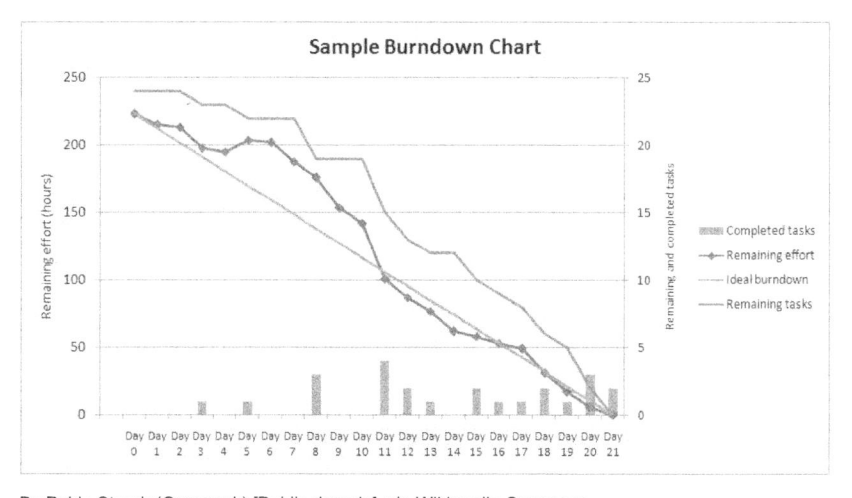

![Sample Burndown Chart]

By Pablo Straub (Own work) [Public domain], via Wikimedia Commons

Through the daily review of the work, it can be determined at an early stage whether the sprint target can be achieved or whether, if necessary, an adjustment of the promised PBIs must be made in cooperation with the product owner.

Sprint Review

In the Sprint Review Meeting the Scrum Team meets with the other stakeholders for a presentation of the increase. The event is time-boxed to 4 hours (based on a sprint of 1 month, proportionally less for shorter sprints). Only fully implemented PBIs are shown, which are included in the increase and thus in the potentially releasable software. What does not meet the requirements of the "Definition of Done" is not considered. The development team and the product owner ensure this together before the Sprint Review.

The Sprint Review Meeting is not a formal acceptance. No signatures are exchanged. It is rather about enabling a structured exchange between the customer and the Scrum team, which leads to a continuous improvement of the result.

The Product Owner shows the status of the Product Backlog and the expected further development.

The whole Scrum team works together on the revision of the product backlog based on customer feedback from the Sprint Review. New PBI can be added, existing ones will be adapted if necessary.

A Sprint Review is performed even if a PBI could not be realized in a Sprint and therefore no new increment could be created. The Sprint Review is seen as an opportunity for optimization and adaptation. Customer feedback can have a significant influence on further planning.

A typical procedure of a Sprint Review Meeting:

1. The Product Owner starts the Sprint Review Meeting and presents the Sprint Goal and what the team has achieved.
2. The Scrum team shows the stakeholders the product increase. It shows how the implementation was planned, how it went, which challenges arose and how these were overcome (or not). Afterwards the Product Increment is gone through and discussed.
3. The Product Owner informs about the current Product Backlog and the expected implementation period.
4. Scrum Team and stakeholders discuss together what should and can be implemented in the next Sprint.

Sprint Retrospective

Like all Scrum events the Sprint Retrospective Meeting is time-boxed. For a monthly sprint it is assumed to be 3 hours, for shorter sprints a proportionally shorter duration. The Sprint

Retrospective is held immediately after the Sprint Review Meeting, before the end of the Sprint. The goal is to optimize the process based on the experiences made.

It is a basic conviction in Scrum that the services provided can always be further improved and that the development process not only affects the resulting software, but also the team and its members. It is clear that the improvement can also relate to smaller issues. The sprint is discussed together and analyzed in terms of contacts, relationships, the process, the means used and the procedures. From this, possibilities for optimization in the next sprint are derived.

Sprint Retrospective is an event in which only members of the Scrum Team participate. Areas where improvement opportunities can be identified are Collaboration, the Scrum process, methods and tools used, product quality, communication, definition of done, etc. It is important to understand that it is about improving the whole team. The whole team is responsible for implementing the agreed improvement goals, not just individual team members.

In practice, Sprint Retrospectives with five steps have proven their worth:

1. Present and honor successes: What went well?

2. Together we will evaluate whether the improvement approaches defined for the current Sprint have been successfully implemented. If they have not been (fully) implemented, it is jointly determined how they can be successfully applied in the next Sprint.
3. The participants gather together where they see room for improvement. Different techniques can be used for this. It is the task of the Scrum Master to ensure that this data collection is done in a constructive, fact-based way.
4. Together, two or three areas are identified in which improvements should be achieved in the upcoming Sprint (this does not concern the product or increment, but the process, which generally also results in an improvement of the Sprint result). It is important not to get bogged down in the choice. It makes more sense to achieve two or three sustainable improvements than to fail at many points. Further approaches can be collected in a Sprint Retrospective Backlog and can be re-themed and prioritized in the following Sprint Retrospectives.
5. It is discussed together how the desired improvement is to be achieved, which conditions are to be fulfilled and how to proceed. Where it is a matter of correcting errors or deficiencies, the reasons that led to them are analyzed and how these errors are to be corrected.

SCRUM ARTIFACTS

Scrum Artifacts

If you read up on different authors, you will find very different information about the number and type of artifacts in Scrum. In fact, the Scrum Manual, which is the basis for the examination, only describes three artifacts. These are Product Backlog, Sprint Backlog and Increment.

product backlog

The Product Backlog is a sorted list of requirements that have been introduced for the final product. These are formulated in simple business language (not technical). They should be understandable for every reader. There should be no interdependencies between requirements. The Product Owner is responsible for prioritizing them and the Product Backlog as a whole. Prioritization in terms of business value is a common aspect, but other bases for prioritization are also conceivable (e.g. legal requirements). All factors together form a value, which is called "Value" or "Importance". Based on this value, the BPIs are ordered by the product owner.

The Product Backlog is continuously developed throughout the entire development process. On the one hand, new requirements may be added, on the other hand, existing requirements are further specified or their effort is reassessed or existing estimates may be adjusted. They are based more on discussions than on written documentation.

The first sprint can be started as soon as a sufficient number of requirements (Product Backlog Items) are available in the Product Backlog, even if they have not yet been described finally. The PBIs in the product backlog must be consistent (they must not contradict each other).

PBIs can be among others:

- Functional requirements
- Non-functional requirements
- New features
- Correction of detected errors and shortcomings
- Technical requirements
- Documentation

PBIs have a Work Estimate, which was created by the development team and is used as the basis for selecting the number of feasible PBIs in a sprint. The work estimates are created as part of the Product Backlog Refinement (also known as Product Backlog grooming) and are adjusted as necessary based on new findings. This work should not require more than 10% of the development team's working time.

Even if a task is implemented by several Scrum teams in parallel, there is only one Product Backlog and one Product Owner.

The project is finished when there are no more open tasks (items) in the product backlog.

Sprint Backlog

The Sprint Backlog is created in the Sprint Planning Meeting. In this meeting the whole Scrum team works together to create the Sprint Backlog. This contains:

- at least one item, possibly several, depending on the estimated implementation time and the capacity of the development team
- A detailed plan of how the items will be implemented during the sprint.

If some elements included in the sprint backlog are not yet completely defined, this can be done in the Product Backlog Refinements during the sprint. In particular it is not possible to define all detailed tasks in the Sprint Planning Meeting. These often only arise during the sprint.

The task of the development team is now to realize the selected items during the sprint according to the criteria of the Definition of Done. The responsibility for the Sprint Backlog lies with the Development Team.

Usually the Sprint Backlog Items remain during the Sprint. However, if the development team determines during the sprint that they have selected too many PBIs or can implement the selected ones faster than expected, the scope can be adjusted in consultation with the product owner.

If several Scrum teams realize a product together and edit PBIs from the same Product Backlog, each Scrum team has its own Sprint Backlog.

product increase

The Product Increment represents the sum of all Product Backlog Items completely (100%) realized at the end of a Sprint. The

Increment must correspond to the definition of "Done" and be potentially releasable. This is also the case if the product owner does not plan to release it.

Product Increments are to be understood cumulatively. Each Increment always includes all features of the previous ones.

If several teams are working on the same product, the increments of the individual teams are combined into one project increment.

IMPORTANT SCRUM TERMS

Product Backlog Refinement

The Product Backlog Refinement is not an own Scrum event but an activity. Accordingly it is not time-boxed. It is sometimes also called Product Backlog Grooming.

The activity includes the review and revision of the Product Backlog Items. Usually, details are added, effort is estimated or effort estimates are adjusted based on new findings and the sequence is adjusted.

The Product Owner is responsible for the prioritization and arrangement of PBIs, the Development Team for the effort estimates.

When the Product Owner adds new PBIs, he explains them to the Development Team and asks them for an estimate of the effort required. This also ensures that the members of the development team know the requirements of the PBIs before the sprint in which they are to be implemented begins. In the Sprint Planning Meeting, the relevant information is simply gone through, adjusted if necessary and supplemented.

The Product Backlog Refinement is neither time-boxed nor is it assigned special times. It takes place during the sprint and may absorb a maximum of 10% of the time available to the development team. It has proven to be a good idea to push the PB Refinement for the next one or two sprints during a sprint. As far as sprint backlog items have not been defined before the sprint as far as necessary for the implementation, they are also processed.

An important task of Product Backlog Refinement is to check the items for consistency. In the course of a project it can happen that requirements change and PBIs arise which contradict each other. This must be verified regularly.

Time Box

The time-box concept is an important basis of Scrum. It forms the basis for focused work in changing conditions. The time-box concept assumes that events are set to a fixed maximum duration in which certain tasks are implemented.

It is possible to adjust the set times for time boxes. However, this should not be done permanently, as each change will lead to the fact that certain empirical values, for example regarding the implementation capacity, will no longer apply.

| Sprint: | max. 1 month (or shorter) |

Sprint Planning:	8 hours for a sprint of 1 month, proportionally less for shorter sprints
Daily Scrum:	15 minutes
Sprint Review:	4 hours for a sprint of 1 month, proportionally less for shorter sprints
Sprint Retrospective:	3 hours for a sprint of 1 month, proportionally less for shorter sprints

Definition of Done

The definition of what exactly is needed for a work package to be considered successfully completed must be agreed upon by the Scrum team at the beginning of the project. It can be continuously refined in the course of the sprints. Only work packages that have been completely implemented and correspond to the common definition (Definition of Done) are included in the Increment and thus in a potentially releasable product.

The Definition of Done usually includes agreements in the following areas:

- Development process (e.g. programming, testing, documentation)

- Non-functional requirements (e.g. security, scalability, maintainability, compatibility)
- Quality and acceptance criteria

If several Scrum teams work on the same project and therefore on the same Product Backlog, it is possible that different teams work with different definitions, for example because they implement different aspects from which different criteria result. In order to create a potentially releasable total increment (one common, not one per team) the different teams must agree on common basic standards. Alternatively, in some cases it is possible to define a company or project wide definition of Done.

Sprint Goal (optional element)

In the Sprint Planning Meeting the Scrum Team defines together the Sprint Goal. It is proposed by the Product Owner, but must be accepted by the whole team. The Sprint Goal is an optional element. It helps the Scrum Team to keep track of its mission for the respective Sprint.

Burn Down Chart

The "Burn Down Chart" (also called "Burn Down Graph") is a graphical representation of the project progress or sprints. For each point in time on the horizontal timeline, the graph shows how much work is/is left to reach the goal at each point in time according to the current estimate. By means of a trend line through the curve based on past estimates, it is possible to predict the probable end of the project or to predict any apparent deviations from the schedule within a sprint and to take countermeasures.

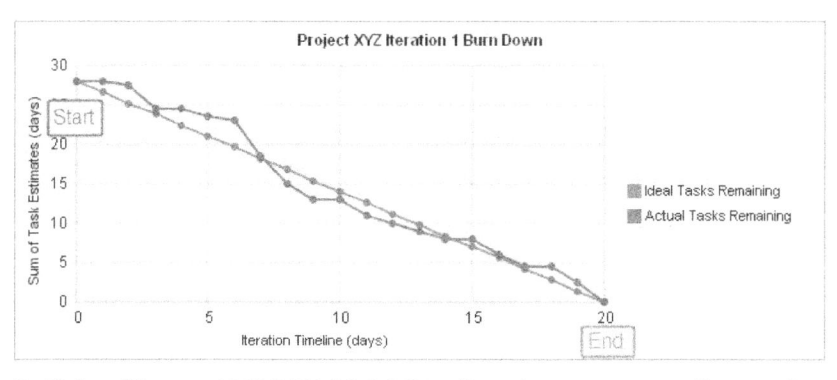

By I8abug (Own work) [CC BY-SA 3.0 (http://creativecommons.org/licenses/by-sa/3.0)], via Wikimedia Commons

TO THE CONCLUSION

I wish you a successful exam and would be pleased if I could support you in this. If you were satisfied with this book, I would be grateful if you could recommend it to friends and rate it online.

We wish you much success

Scrum On!

Score PASS
       78 points scored (or 97.5%) out of 80 maximum points
       (a score of 85.0% or greater is needed to pass this test)

Summary of Results By Section

The questions in this test were organized by section. This table details a summary of your scores by section.

Section/Subject Area	Percentage Scored
Scrum Framework - Rules and roles of Scrum per the Scrum Guide.	97.5%
Scrum Theory and Principles - Good understanding of Scrum theory, how it is founded on empirical theory, and the principles and values of Scrum.	95.0%
Cross-functional, self-organizing Teams - Scrum Teams are different from traditional development groups. The paradigm and nature of a cross-functional and self-organizing team promotes flexibility, creativity, and productivity. They choose how to best do their work and have all competencies needed to accomplish it without depending on others outside of the team.	100.0%
Coaching & Facilitation - Overall behavior of Scrum Masters are very different from project managers or team leaders in	100.0%